W9-BZT-789

~ 50 ~
WRITING LESSONS
THAT WORK!

Motivating prompts
and easy activities
that develop the
essentials of
strong writing

By Carol Rawlings Miller

SCHOLASTIC
PROFESSIONAL BOOKS

New York • Toronto • London • Auckland • Sydney
Mexico City • New Delhi • Hong Kong

Dedication

To Elizabeth McMillen, my grandmother, who taught school for a quarter of a century in West Virginia. She brought her love of teaching to all kinds of classrooms, including a one-room schoolhouse.

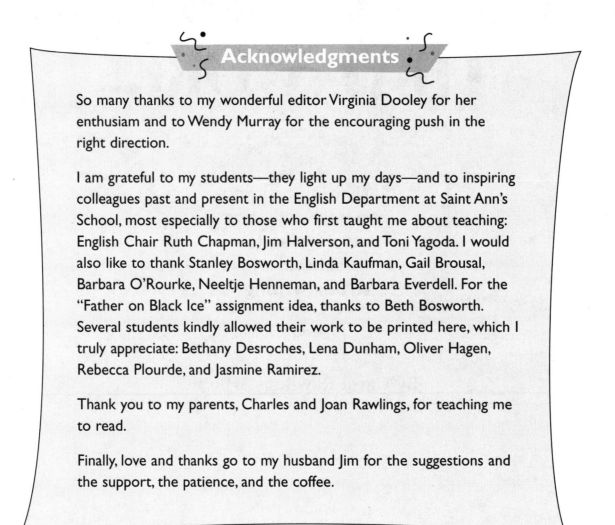

Acknowledgments

So many thanks to my wonderful editor Virginia Dooley for her enthusiam and to Wendy Murray for the encouraging push in the right direction.

I am grateful to my students—they light up my days—and to inspiring colleagues past and present in the English Department at Saint Ann's School, most especially to those who first taught me about teaching: English Chair Ruth Chapman, Jim Halverson, and Toni Yagoda. I would also like to thank Stanley Bosworth, Linda Kaufman, Gail Brousal, Barbara O'Rourke, Neeltje Henneman, and Barbara Everdell. For the "Father on Black Ice" assignment idea, thanks to Beth Bosworth. Several students kindly allowed their work to be printed here, which I truly appreciate: Bethany Desroches, Lena Dunham, Oliver Hagen, Rebecca Plourde, and Jasmine Ramirez.

Thank you to my parents, Charles and Joan Rawlings, for teaching me to read.

Finally, love and thanks go to my husband Jim for the suggestions and the support, the patience, and the coffee.

"Father on Black Ice" by Nancy White from *Sun, Moon, Salt* published by Word Works. Used by permission of the poet.

Cover design by Jaime Lucero
Interior design by Sydney Wright
Interior photographs by Oi Pin Chan, and Greg Gilbert
ISBN 0-590-52212-4

Copyright © 1999 by Carol Rawlings Miller. All rights reserved.
Printed in the U.S.A.

Contents

Introduction 5

Part 1: Paragraphs 〜

Portrait Writing: supporting a generalization 8

That's So Annoying: creating focus with a clear topic sentence 9

Moody Weather: using vivid details 10

It's in the Details: using vivid details 11

Lingering Mood: using similes 11

Haiku Honey: attuning students to language, rhythm, and image 12

Fantasy Living: using fanciful details 13

Dueling Insults: using language in inventive, enjoyable ways 13

Many Beginnings: building writing stamina 14

Strong Finishes: writing conclusions 15

Our Town: stating an opinion .16

Controversy!: supporting an argument with facts 16

A How-to Paragraph for Aliens: writing clear instructions 17

Sum It Up!: writing a summary 18

Listen Up!: building listening skills 18

One-of-a-Kind Character: analyzing a literary character 19

Reproducibles:

What Is a Paragraph? 21

It's in the Details 22

Story Starters for "Many Beginnings" 23

Part 2: Linking Paragraphs 〜

Home, Sweet Home, Inside and Out: using transitional devices 25

Of the Four Seasons: creating transitions between contrasting paragraphs 26

A Spooky Place, Out and In: linking paragraphs in creative pieces 26

In Order: using transitions to show sequence 27

Crafting Transitions: using transitional techniques 28

Follow Up: making smooth transitions 29

TV Watching—the Pros and Cons: making an analysis 29

Reproducibles:

Transitions 31

Unscramble the Sentences 32

Follow Up 34

Part 3: Full Compositions 〜

Fallen Hero: developing a personal essay 35

Family Photograph: building storytelling skills .36

Autobiography: using vignettes in a composition 37

Variety is the Spice of Life: avoiding repetition 38

Playing With Sentences: using different kinds of sentences 38

Sheer Excitement: writing sentences in a vivid and interesting way 39

What Is?: using a quotation to shape an essay .39

Beautiful Dreamer: using a verbal refrain to shape a piece 40

What's in a Meal?: creating atmosphere 41

The In-Class Journal: thinking on paper 41

So Far Away: creating a believable character 42

The Prophecy: developing a strong plot 43

Children's Storybook: focusing on plot and writing for a specific audience 44

Nightlife: establishing a setting 44

Story in a Poem of Short Lines: writing a poem that tells a story 45

Mystery Egg: writing with a particular audience in mind 46

Dialogue with Sentence Focus: using correct dialogue form 46

Finders Keepers: using play structure 47

Confess!: writing a first-person narrative 48

Stream of Consciousness: developing a voice 48

Same Theme, Different Reader: experimenting with diction 49

An Essay on Meaning: revising an essay 50

Please Change: writing a formal letter 50

Job Application: writing a job application letter 51

The Food Critic: making and organizing an evaluation 52

Blueprint for the Future: making and using an outline 53

Halloween Reflection: organizing and outlining ideas 54

The Literary Essay: using the text as evidence .55

Reproducibles:

The Essay 56

Variety is the Spice of Life 57

Playing with Sentences 58

"Father on Black Ice" by Nancy White 60

A Formal Letter 64

Introduction

~ Why This Book? ~

Teaching writing seems simple enough: we need to help our students improve. Being responsible for their writing skills, however, can seem overwhelming. Writing is nothing if not complex, student problems are varied, and often we can only guess at what ground they have already covered in school. Finally, across the nation, students are taking more standardized tests that include writing. As they sit in our classrooms, we feel more keenly than ever that they need to make discernible progress.

And yet, in spite of these legitimate concerns, we cannot and should not teach writing with grim determination. We are shaping how students approach writing. In fact, we want them to learn to love writing because finding joy in expression can have everything to do with their writing confidently and well. Students should be engaged by writing, and if they have positive experiences that ignite their imaginations and respect their natural intelligence, they will be.

The intention of this book is to provide you with assignments that can help you keep your students writing frequently, purposefully, and happily. To become flexible, inventive writers, students need the spice of life: a variety of assignments that build all kinds of skills, work against mechanical writing, and give them a range of compositional experiences. This book exposes students to different genres of creative, critical, and personal writing.

~ The Premise ~

The overarching premise of this book is that the student who can paragraph well can write, and that it is in the service of building the intelligent, compelling writer that students do both expository and creative pieces. The first part of the book provides numerous paragraphing assignments; the next part teaches students to link paragraphs and build transitions; the final section is devoted to full compositions. Poetry assignments have been included to enhance overall awareness of language. All of these assignments are designed to promote focused, developed writing, but other skills are addressed, too, including pre-writing skills (learning to brainstorm, gather ideas, and outline), making strong word choices, using sentence variety, and employing diction wisely.

Why should students do both expository and creative assignments? The expository writer who can create paragraph focus, organize and develop ideas thoroughly, and link paragraphs effectively has learned skills absolutely essential to good writing. In concert with this, working on creative assignments encourages students to use language imaginatively and to trust and learn about their voices; the discipline of the essay sometimes works against expressiveness and experimentation. Too much expository writing can lead to a flat, unconfident voice and a mechanical sense of structure. Too much creative writing can leave students at sea when it comes to the discipline of making an argument in an essay.

~ How to Use this Book ~

Assignment instructions are written so that they can be copied directly onto the board for student use. Each assignment has a specific skills focus, but you should always encourage students to incorporate all the writing skills they are acquiring in each new piece of writing they do.

While the assignments by section move from discrete paragraphing prompts to full composition assignments, you may not want to move through the book in order. In terms of building writing stamina, it is probably better for students to go back and forth between shorter and longer assignments: short assignments allow students to work very closely on focus and structure; longer assignments let them have experience organizing and developing ideas at length. However, if you have students who are new, inexperienced, or unfocused writers, place more emphasis on the paragraphing assignments at first, which are less intimidating, and introduce longer assignments as soon as it seems feasible.

～ A Few Thoughts on Teaching Writing ～

Learning to write is challenging and sometimes difficult for children, so they need encouragement and applause, even for small gains like remembering to indent. Praise is not, of course, all they need. They also need focused suggestions that will not overwhelm or depress them; you want to point them in a very clear, understandable direction. Consider giving them two or three focused pointers at the end of each assignment. If you are saddled with very large classes and cannot reasonably grade an assignment a week, you can keep students writing between fully graded assignments with focused journal work. Students learn to write by doing; don't let your inability to mark an assignment every week get in their way. Journal writing can meet something of their need for constant writing experience without jeopardizing your sanity with an inhuman amount of grading.

For all of you who are up early and late marking papers, I hope these assignments ease your way. Teaching writing is consuming work, and, as we all know, sometimes it can seem like a thankless task. Still, I believe what we do truly is important; we help students discover a voice on paper, which is, to me, another form of being able to vote. And finally, we get to work with the most incredibly fine and inspiring tools: the human mind, the imagination, and language.

Part 1

Paragraphs

PORTRAIT WRITING

Skills Focus: to support a generalization with vivid details

Assignment: In one well-developed paragraph, describe the personality of an individual you know and like very much.

Ask students to convey this person's character and essence. This person might be fun or funny or sweet or kind or intriguing (or all or none of these). A reader should, by the end of the paragraph, have a sharp sense of an individual personality—of how someone thinks and acts, what he or she looks like, and how the writer feels about that person. Remind students that details are extremely important here. If they write about a grandmother, a reader should see beyond a stereotype like "nice old lady." Even if Grandma is nice and old, she is more than that, just as students are more than "good kids." Encourage them to relate vignettes that illustrate personality.

Warm Up: Discuss different ways to approach writing topic sentences. Emphasize that students should begin with a clear generalization about personality. In the body, they should support this generalization with brief stories and relevant details, such as physical descriptions.

Teaching Tip

A student may wish to write about someone they dislike; if you allow this, tell them that a reader should not be able to recognize that person. Siblings, friends at school, teachers, or administrators are not good subjects.

Follow Up: Have volunteers read aloud their paragraphs. Ask students if they were curious about anything that the writer did not communicate about the person. This will help writers think about the depth and detail of their writing.

THAT'S SO ANNOYING

Skills Focus: to create focus with a clear topic sentence

Assignment: Write about something that annoys you; use details that convey fully why this is so bothersome.

Suggest that students think of trying family events, dull routines or chores, jam-packed stores, lackluster entertainment, or shoddy products (especially toys or candy). Tell them that they should be so specific that their readers should feel something, too, such as irritation, amusement, or both.

Warm Up: Think of something universally delightful to your students such as ice cream or amusement parks. With students, brainstorm the things that are wonderful about ice cream or amusement parks; write their responses on the board in a word web so they can see the specific details.

After reviewing paragraph structure, have the class compose a great topic sentence: move them away from the overly general or bland (such as "Ice cream is great") to something more specific and interesting (such as "Creamy, smooth, and sweet, ice cream in its many varieties is the perfect solution to life's little troubles"). Discuss how the topic sentence gives the writer somewhere to go.

Teaching Tip

Students enjoy this opportunity to say what they really think; let them do so without unnecessary censure. Your support for their honesty will build their trust in you as a reader and promote the development of an interesting and individual voice. Students who write too cautiously do not write well.

MOODY WEATHER

Skills Focus: to use vivid details to connect feelings and environment

Assignment: Write a first-person paragraph about the weather today and how it makes you feel. Before you write, observe and think. How does it look outside? What mood does this weather put you in?

For this assignment choose a day that is somehow notable: foggy and tired, or blustery and nervous-feeling, and so on. Urge students to think for a moment about how this weather makes them feel. Tell them to think of the day as an individual; it might be bright blue out, but what is particular to this day? How does it smell: new and green, like fresh-cut grass from the park? What is the wind like? Is it bringing the smells from a nearby factory their way?

Warm Up: Before they begin, remind students of paragraph structure. They should write a strong topic sentence. Suggest that they begin with a generalization about the type of day it is and how it makes them feel. Place additional emphasis here on the five senses: taste, touch, sight, smell, and hearing. Remind students that great writing appeals to a reader's senses.

Read aloud some models of good weather descriptions. For snow see the last paragraph of James Joyce's "The Dead" or the beginning of Joan Aiken's *The Wolves of Willoughby Chase*; for a description of fall try Chapter 14 of Elizabeth George Speare's *The Witch of Blackbird Pond*.

Follow Up: Have students read aloud their paragraphs and draw them into discussion about how different the pieces are. Introduce them to the idea of subjectivity: to varying degrees, we do not think alike. Students benefit from exploring what the idea of truth in writing means. We may witness the same event but have different viewpoints or interpretations of it. Have them discuss what causes this. Do we ever hear, or tell, "just the facts"?

Three Student Samples Written on the Same Day:

With no clouds in the sky it is still subtly cloudy. I can see no sun, but yet it is bright. On a day like today I feel calm, as all I can hear is the buzzing of city street cleaners. The sky, although lit by the unseen sun, is a pale off-white. The sounds of the city only add to this calming effect, and, with the familiar buildings surrounding and setting a place for the sky, I feel at home.

—Bethany, seventh grade

It was a city morning, early in the winter, and unusually warm and humid. The sky was white and swollen, and the slanted brick and slate rooms stood out starkly against it. The smoke that rose from the factory buildings could be seen in the distance. The streets were empty, and the occasional body carried an umbrella in anticipation of the probable rain. The morning was quiet and every sound echoed through the street as if it were bouncing off the buildings in a ball. The only steady sound was the low hum of a garbage truck picking up the bags off the sidewalk and loading onto an ever-growing pile. —*Lena, seventh grade*

I'm getting a big fat headache right now sitting here being bored in class, looking out the window and seeing a gloomy sky and wondering if it'll rain. Inside, there is a smell and awareness of a stuffy car and its exhaust fumes, while outside, it is a little chilly, but yet moist. It makes you feel all tired out and wanting to sleep. Still, it's a nice day, but only outside. When inside on this day, the most refreshing thing is the outside air. The air comes into your nose and has its own distinct smell. I love the sense of fresh air in the room, it clears you up and makes you feel good. There is a pigeon on the stoop, enjoying the air while I have to be sitting here in class bored. There is a sense of urgency to be outdoors, which is not being attended to. I wish it was 10:10. —*Oliver, seventh grade*

IT'S IN THE DETAILS

Skills Focus: to use vivid details

Assignment: Follow the directions on *It's in the Details* to complete the page.

Using the reproducible *It's in the Details* (page 22), have students explore the way details create images in the reader's mind. Some details help give us important facts. For example, the paragraph from *Johnny Tremain* tells us essential facts, like his age and his appearance. Novels and stories need to describe characters carefully. The Harper Lee paragraph has incredible images that create a sense of atmosphere, like the simile for the ladies: "like soft teacakes with frostings of sweat and sweet talcum."

LINGERING MOOD

Skills Focus: to use similes to describe a place

Assignment: Describe the mood in a room or another place right after people have just left it; pretend you are peeking in through a crack in the wall. This could be a dining room, a classroom, a theater, a place of worship, or somewhere else. What does the room look and feel like at the moment when it is empty again. Does it feel peaceful? Stirred up? Does anything indicate that people have just been there: if you stumbled upon the room, would you know people had just left, or not? Use similes in your description.

When students describe a room that has been left, encourage them to use interesting word choices and similes (comparisons beginning them with "like" or "as").

Warm Up: Read the following simile from *Bridge to Terabithia* to students:

> "…her pale brown hair stuck up all over her head like a squirrel's nest on a winter branch."

Discuss the way this comparison brings a strong image to mind. Encourage students to avoid clichés in their similes.

HAIKU HONEY

Skills Focus: to attune students to language, rhythm, and image

Assignment: Write a series of five to ten haiku. Because this will be a "series" there should be some unifying theme or element (like seasons or an exploration of different emotions). There do not need to be transitions between the different haiku. Each haiku should have one or two wonderfully vivid images.

Warm Up: You will need to introduce your students to haiku, which you can easily do on the blackboard. (See below.) After you show them some haiku, then write one or two together on the board. First, pick a topic, like spring or love, and then ask them to imagine an image that communicates the essence of spring. On the board, as you compose together, pay close attention to counting syllables. Applaud all ideas, but push them to keep coming up with ideas until you have something interesting. Discourage clichés.

Haiku is a Japanese form that is three lines long and has, usually, seventeen syllables (the first line has five, the second seven, and the third five).

In haiku the writer usually creates one strong image, and oftentimes there is some seasonal reference or reference to the weather and/or the time of day.

Examples:

> For the child who won't
> stop crying, she lights a lamp
> in the autumn dusk
> *Kawahigashi Kekigodo (1837-1937)*

> A lightning gleam:
> into darkness travels
> a night heron's scream.
> *Matsuo Bashu (1644-1694)*

> To the sun's paths
> the hollyhocks lean
> in the May rains.

Follow-Up: Read or copy for them some famous haiku series composed in English, like the modern poet Wallace Stevens's "Thirteen Ways of Looking at a Blackbird" or Etheridge Knight's jazzy haiku series called "Haiku."

FANTASY LIVING

Skills Focus: to use fanciful details

Assignment: Write one or two long paragraphs in which you describe a fantasy room—think of your favorite kind of room. The description can be as wild and fanciful as you want. Feel free to invent machines and gizmos that do not and cannot exist.

Begin the assignment by reading aloud to students a detailed, fantastic description. My students have responded well to the description of a bathroom from F. Scott Fitzgerald's short story "The Diamond as Big as the Ritz." This passage is often incredibly stimulating for students; don't be surprised if you hear echoes of Fitzgerald in their pieces (writing after models is a terrific way to learn).

Warm Up: On the board, write the five senses—taste, smell, touch, sight, hearing. Tell students that their writing should excite and please the reader's senses; the reader should be swept away or amazed by the wonderful rooms they describe. Encourage students to have fun with this assignment.

Discussion: After students read their pieces aloud (students love to share them), start a discussion of the word *imagination*. Have a student look up the word in the dictionary and read aloud the definition. Ask the class where they think ideas come from. And why, do they suppose, do people love fantasy so much?

DUELING INSULTS

Skills Focus: to use language in inventive, enjoyable ways

Assignment: Write a story in which two characters are trading very original insults. Before you begin, think over what they are arguing about (money, love, schoolwork, friends). And be sure to use proper dialogue form. Get as nasty and mean in these insults as possible but do not use curse words; they're too easy.

To get students going ask them for some common insults, like "pea brain" or "spineless." Talk to them about making the insults precise and personal. They can be whole sentences, like "You're so boring even your mother falls asleep when you talk," or two-word phrases, like "human sedative."

You might tell them some of Shakespeare's gloriously specific insults, like "glass-gazer" or "you bead, you acorn," or "you canker blossom."

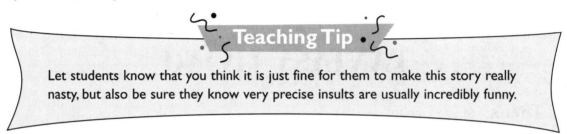

Teaching Tip

Let students know that you think it is just fine for them to make this story really nasty, but also be sure they know very precise insults are usually incredibly funny.

Follow Up: Students will love to read these pieces out loud, so don't hold them back; it should be great fun. Also, a discussion about clichés naturally follows this assignment. Put some romantic clichés on the board and have students try to come up with more original ideas: *heart-stopping, her eyes were like pools of blue, sweet as a rose, dew-kissed, pretty as a picture,* and so on.

MANY BEGINNINGS

Skills Focus: to build writing stamina

Assignment: By the end of this assignment, you should have seven story beginnings. Here's how the assignment works. You will receive a slip of paper that contains the first line of a story. Copy down the line on a sheet of paper and then continue the story. Write quickly, and don't worry too much about what you're writing.

You'll work on that story for about five minutes, until I tell you to stop. Then pass the slip of paper to the next student; you'll receive a new slip of paper from another student. Skip two lines, copy down the new line, and start a new story! You should not connect the stories at all; each story beginning should stand on its own.

The first lines for the stories are on the reproducible, *Many Beginnings* (see pages 23-24); copy the pages and cut them into slips. Tell students that they will probably need two sheets of paper for their stories. Also, you will need to clarify to whom they should pass their slips of paper.

Teaching Tip

Present this assignment with a lot of enthusiasm and energy. At first let students write for about five minutes or until you see that everyone has a paragraph or so. After the first change of slips, check around the room and make sure everyone is on track; sometimes students think they are supposed to link the stories. You might want to bring in a timer; the loud ding creates a little nervous excitement. And by all means, urge students to write quickly; lash them along in a humorous way. They'll be proud of how much they've written by the end of the assignment.

Follow Up: Mark these pieces with a light hand since they were done in a very uncontrolled manner. You want to praise students for how much they wrote and applaud their ideas and images. Have them read aloud their favorite story starters. A natural extension of this assignment is, of course, to ask students to choose their favorite beginnings and write stories with them.

STRONG FINISHES

Skills Focus: to write strong concluding sentences

Assignment: Your school administration has decided to institute a new homework policy. From now on, each weekday students will be required to complete three hours of homework, and each weekend a total of four hours. Write a paragraph telling how you and your fellow students feel about this new policy.

Discuss the importance of writing a strong concluding sentence with your students. Explain that a writer often ends a paragraph with a sentence that returns to the basic theme—but in light of the facts reviewed in the body. Introduce students to phrases such as "in conclusion" and "in light of this evidence," but also emphasize that these phrases can sound overly formulaic. Younger students unfamiliar with these terms should learn them. Older students may need to learn about other ways to conclude such as making a twist on the topic sentence or referring in summation to the facts addressed.

Warm Up: Read the following paragraph aloud to your students.

I object to the new town council law that prohibits anyone from riding bicycles within the town's borders. More than 45% of the town's residents own bicycles, and many of these bicycle owners use them to commute to work and school. Since I do not own a car, the bicycle prohibition law means that I will have to walk to school. It will now take me three times as long to travel back and forth to school.

Ask students if the piece seems finished, or do they feel that they are still in the middle of learning about something. Ask volunteers for ideas about how to end the paragraph.

Follow Up: Have students look at another piece of writing they've done. If a piece needs help and a student is willing, ask other students for ideas on how to end the paragraph. Write their ideas on the board. While a student could do this, it will probably be easier, quicker, and clearer if you record the ideas on the board.

OUR TOWN

Skills Focus: to state an opinion

Assignment: Write a paragraph that takes a stand on this question:

Is your home town/city/area/neighborhood a good place to live?

Back up your opinion. Explain why you think what you think, but do not use the first person.

Encourage students to state their opinions very clearly in their topic sentences. They should have clear and compelling examples that would persuade someone that they are right. Encourage students to write well-developed paragraphs; the paragraph should neither be too long (so many sentences that it needs to break off into a new paragraph), nor should it be too short (a few sentences that only thinly develop the topic sentence).

Warm Up: Do some writing on the board with the class. Ask students to make generalizations about something simple and handy such as their school desks or their pens. Write a topic sentence on the board such as "The Good Write Pen is a good pen." Ask for ideas about how to make that topic sentence more precise and more interesting. To reinforce their grasp of paragraph structure, ask students what ideas back up the generalization in the topic sentence. List their ideas on the board.

CONTROVERSY!

Skills Focus: to support an argument with facts

Assignment: Take a stand on a controversial topic. Support your argument with facts and convince your reader that you are right. Do not use the first person.

There are a range of topics you might suggest, and obviously not all topics work well everywhere. Here are some questions you might have students consider:

★ Should kids be able to get tattoos without parental permission?

* ★ Are school uniforms a good idea or a bad one?
* ★ Should smoking be illegal for everyone?
* ★ Should Americans support NASA with tax dollars?
* ★ Should people be required by law to vote?
* ★ Should school be held year-round?
* ★ Should kids have total access to the Internet?

Warm Up: First prepare students for writing by having them take notes. 1) Tell everyone to select a question and write it at the top of a sheet of paper. 2) Then students should skip two lines and write their general answers to the question; this will be the basis of their topic sentence. 3) They should jot down a list of reasons. Give students several minutes to compile their lists. Explain that they should use the lists to help them write the bodies of their paragraphs.

Then have students write a paragraph using their notes. Inform students that the topic sentence should not only be a clear response to the question, but it should also give a sense of "why." For example, "Main Street should definitely be closed to cars on the weekend so that everyone can walk easily from shop to shop without living in fear of the traffic."

A HOW-TO PARAGRAPH FOR ALIENS

Skills Focus: to write clear instructions

Assignment: An alien wants to imitate you! First, it needs information. Write a note to the alien that in one paragraph gives clear instructions on how to get ready for school. The alien should be able to impersonate you exactly and not get caught.

This assignment asks students to think over something that is second nature to them; they must break down actions and describe them. Students must not only think about what they do but how they do it: are they grumpy in the morning, or do they spring out of bed? They should have fun with this assignment; encourage them to come up with good names for their alien.

Warm Up: Discuss putting on shoes: how would students write instructions for this activity? Make a list, in order, of the actions that must take place for a person to be successfully shod. Look over the list together, checking sequence and making sure the actions are listed in the proper order.

Follow Up: Talk about why it is so hard to write good instructions. You might suggest that students ask their parents for examples of bad instructions that have come with some products. Oftentimes, words or steps are left out, which leaves the reader at a loss. Not only do students love to see these mistakes made in the adult world, but examples of poor writing show them the impression that sloppiness creates—and the unfortunate results.

SUM IT UP!

Skills Focus: to write a summary of a chapter

Assignment: Write a one-paragraph summary of Chapter _____. This summary should provide a sense of what happens in the chapter; if a reader lost this chapter of the book, your summary could help him or her go on to the next chapter without getting confused.

Tell students that their paragraphs should not exceed seven sentences. They should read the chapter over (some may only need to skim) and trace what happens. Remind them to take note of significant changes in mood and setting. The paragraph should be organized chronologically; it should echo the order of action in the chapter. The paragraph should not be too detailed; on the other hand, if a detail or image is highlighted by the author, it should be part of the summary.

Note: This assignment is simple, but it can be enormously revealing about how well a student is reading. Furthermore, being able to summarize is one of the most crucial cognitive skills; it forces students to synthesize, choose, and condense. In addition, being able to summarize is useful in every discipline. I tell students that they should write a short summary of any chapter in science or history when they are confused; this helps them pinpoint what they do not understand, which allows them to come to a teacher with specific questions rather than with vague and hard-to-address complaints.

LISTEN UP!

Skills Focus: to build listening skills

Assignment: Listen to the short story I am going to read. Afterwards you will write an informal summary of it.

Many standardized tests include sections in which students respond to a selection that is read to them. To build listening skills, read aloud a short story to students. For younger students, read *Rikki-Tikki-Tavi* by Rudyard Kipling or "The Red-Headed League" by Sir Arthur Conan Doyle. For older students, Ernest Hemingway's "Three Shots" and "Indian Camp" work well together; or read "The Tell-Tale Heart" by Edgar Allan Poe. Tell students that you're going to ask them to write an informal summary after you finish reading ("informal" because you want to avoid having students listen too anxiously). If this feels more like a game than a serious assignment, you may get better results.

Huck and Jim encountered some fog, and Huck got lost in the middle of it all. So when he finally found Jim again, he was saying how he never got lost. Then he told Jim he had never seen any fog or any islands, and that he had been speaking to him for ten minutes and he was drunk. Jim then goes on talking about how a true friend wouldn't lie about sleeping, so he really got angry with Huck and started yelling at him.
                                                                                                —*Jasmine, seventh grade*

ONE-OF-A-KIND CHARACTER

Skills Focus: to analyze a literary character

Assignment: In one well-structured paragraph describe a character from the book. Reveal the character's personality and his or her situation in the book. Use examples and quotations to support your topic sentence.

Have students use this assignment for a book they are reading. For homework, have students first take some notes. They should write a generalization at the top of the page and then some notes that include at least two examples and two quotations that explain the generalization. They should include the page numbers on which they found the quotations. In class the next day, check over students' notes and then have them write the paragraph. Have them refer to the *What Is a Paragraph?* reproducible (page 21) to remind them of how to proceed. Discourage students from beginning only with a physical description, unless that is the topic.

Warm Up: To show students how to take notes, write this format on the board:

Generalization: At the beginning of *Abel's Island* by William Steig, Abel is used to the very best of everything. In fact, he seems to be spoiled. Still, Abel is likable.

page 4: Abel's lunch is filled with expensive ingredients like caviar and champagne.

page 4: Abel gives a daisy umbrella to his wife.

page 6: When the picnic is rained on, Abel gets into a huff. He is "offended at the thoughtless weather."

Tell students that to write well about a book they should think like a lawyer; they need to find evidence to back up their ideas. No lawyer would say, "My client is innocent" without evidence. No jury would be convinced by vagueness. To find this "evidence," students need first to do some thinking and re-reading; they need to discover what they think and why they think it. This legal analogy is extremely effective. The idea that a lawyer would assert innocence without proof can sound amusingly preposterous, but do make the point that their writing should not sound "legal."

Student Sample:

In *The Witch of Blackbird Pond* by Elizabeth George Speare, Goodwife Cruff is a very mean person. She hardly feeds Prudence, and she told her she was too stupid and too old to be in the town's school. Also, she abuses her child by making her stand up and watch her and her husband eat. The father is a little nicer, but not much; occasionally he slips her a morsel of food when Goodwife Cruff isn't looking. All the scenes in this book that Goodwife Cruff is in really give you a good impression of how cruel and nasty she is.

—*Rebecca, fifth grade*

What Is a Paragraph?

A paragraph is a unit of writing, a group of sentences that all work together. A paragraph has a beginning, a middle, and an end.

∼ The Expository Paragraph ∼

In an essay, a paragraph is made up of three parts.

I. Topic Sentence

The topic sentence states what the paragraph is about. The statement should be clear and interesting. The topic sentence is usually the first sentence, but it may appear later in the paragraph.

II. Body

The body includes all the sentences that go between the topic sentence and the concluding sentence. In the body you explain the topic in detail and back up what you say with examples.

III. Concluding Sentence

The concluding sentence wraps up what you want to say in the paragraph. If it is the last sentence of a paper, it should leave the reader feeling that the idea is complete. If another paragraph follows, the concluding sentence may also help create a transition to the next paragraph.

∼ The Creative Writing Paragraph ∼

In a story, there are many different kinds of paragraphs.

In a story, you start a new paragraph when the focus shifts, something new happens, or there is a change of place, time, subject, or mood. Also, when writing dialogue, you indent, or start a new paragraph, each time the speaker changes. The nature of the paragraph's beginning, middle, and end is usually different in a story than it is in an essay; a story might not have a topic sentence. In a story, you often create the focus of a paragraph by developing ideas through very specific language.

It's in the Details

Read the paragraphs below and then answer the questions on another sheet of paper.

"Johnny was already in his leather breeches, pulling on his coarse shirt, tucking in the tails. He was a rather skinny boy, neither large nor small for fourteen. He had a thin, sleep-flushed face, light eyes, a wry mouth, and fair, lank hair. Although two years younger than the swinish Dove, inches shorter, pounds lighter, he knew, and old Mr. Lapham knew, busy Mrs. Lapham and her four daughters and Dusty and Dove also knew, that Johnny Tremain was the boss of the attic, and almost of the house." —from *Johnny Tremain* by Esther Forbes

"Maycomb was an old town, but it was a tired old town when I first knew it. In rainy weather the streets turned to red slop; grass grew on the sidewalks, the courthouse sagged in the square. Somehow, it was hotter then: a black dog suffered on a summer's day; bony mules hitched to Hoover carts flicked flies in the sweltering shade of the live oaks on the square. Men's stiff collars wilted by nine in the morning. Ladies bathed before noon, after their three-o'clock naps, and by nightfall were like soft teacakes with frostings of sweat and sweet talcum."   —from *To Kill a Mockingbird* by Harper Lee

1. What makes these examples hang together as paragraphs?

2. What effect do the details create?

Look at the two paragraphs below. Why did the author start a new paragraph after the first one?

"Silence fell between them, as tangible as the dark tree shadows that fell across their laps and now seemed to rest upon them heavily as though they possessed a measurable weight of their own. At last Calvin spoke in a dry, unemotional voice, not looking at Meg.

'Do you think he could be dead?'"

—from *A Wrinkle in Time* by Madeleine L'Engle

Story Starters for "Many Beginnings"

Copy and cut these first lines into separate slips. Distribute one line to each student.

After a long drive, old Mr. Dingleson always liked to clean the exterior of his car until it was spit spot.

Listening to the weather report on the police radio, the family huddled around a candle in the dark house.

The younger students, with their whining and their unzipped jackets, were driving him/her crazy.

The arrival of an alien at dinner was not something Jeffrey could figure out how to explain. Where should he begin?

Eliza winced whenever her mother tried to speak in a "hip" way.

Rage built in her/him.

Sweetie Jenkins had always flown first class with her Mummy and Daddy.

The sound of the far-off train whistle made the gloomy night seem even scarier.

The children realized anxiously that the tide was coming in.

Janey hid under the old tractor, staring at the huge muddy wheel, plotting her revenge.

Story Starters for "Many Beginnings"

I like to irritate people so very, very much.

Even though the aromas of the little house were overwhelmingly wonderful, she still felt . . .

Late-night laughter on a city street always made her nervous.

Given the fact that cavities were being filled just feet away, the receptionist in the dentist's office seemed far too happy.

It depressed him/her, the way his mother sat in the light of the computer all day. Why was his/her sister so embarrassing?

Standing in the hot sun, waiting for Super Express, the fastest roller coaster in the world, Hannah felt certain that she would . . .

Falling in love had once seemed so ridiculous, but now . . .

Linking Paragraphs

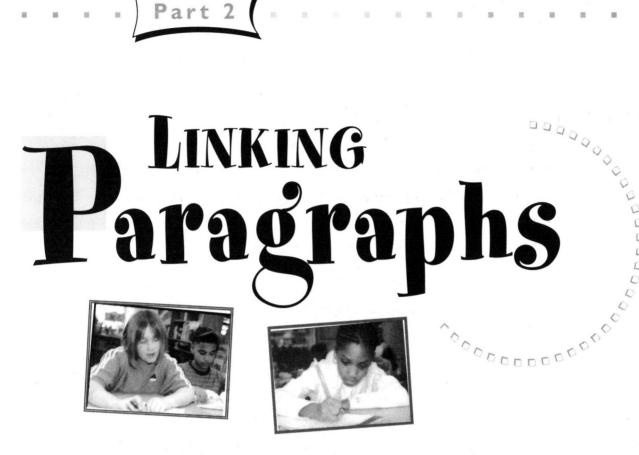

. . HOME, SWEET HOME, INSIDE AND OUT

Skills Focus: to use transitional devices

Assignment: Write two sharply focused paragraphs about the place where you live: one about the outside environment, one about the inside environment. Write about them in whichever order you like—but before you begin, you should observe.

Try to give students a sense of the questions they might consider for each paragraph.

The Outside: Students should look at where their homes are situated and consider the actual feeling of the locations. Is the location bustling? Sleepy? Isolated? Tell them to think about the elements that generate the feeling of the locations.

The Inside: Students should look around their homes and describe the atmospheres of their living situations. Again, tell them to first look carefully. Through details, a reader should get a good sense of who lives there.

Warm Up: After reminding them about writing strong topic sentences, go over transitional devices with students (see *Transitions*, page 31).

OF THE FOUR SEASONS

Skills Focus: to create transitions between contrasting paragraphs

Assignment: In two linked paragraphs, write about two seasons. Explain which season you like the most and which season you like least.

Before they begin, ask students to suggest the best way to organize their paragraphs. Steer them to the idea of creating paragraph coherence and writing about one season at a time.

In order to help students write fully developed paragraphs, have them think of all the things they can write about. What can they do at certain times of year that they cannot do during other seasons? What is the weather like? Remind students to appeal to all of the reader's senses: what seasonal smells, sights, and sounds make them feel as they do?

Warm Up: Highlight the transition inherent between the two paragraphs; you may want to do this after students have written the first paragraph at home. Go over transitional terms on the board (see *Transitions* reproducible, page 31), underscoring words and phrases useful for making contrasts: on the other hand, conversely, on the contrary, unlike, instead, whereas. Students might want to use an if/then construction. Write the following sentences on the board:

"If soccer practice is the joy of my life, then doing my chores is the bane of my existence."

"If I look forward to visiting my cousins, I dread the annual trip to Great Aunt Snarky."

Ask students what each sentence implies about the topics of paragraphs one and two.

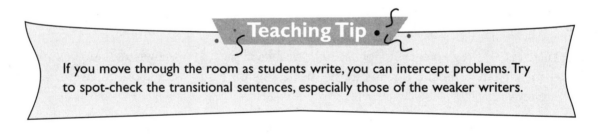

Teaching Tip

If you move through the room as students write, you can intercept problems. Try to spot-check the transitional sentences, especially those of the weaker writers.

A SPOOKY PLACE, OUT AND IN

Skills Focus: to link paragraphs in creative pieces

Assignment: For this assignment, you'll write in the first person. Make yourself a character in the story or create a character who narrates it. Write two very detailed paragraphs about a haunted place. It could be a house or a building or a natural place, like a cave or a forest. In your first paragraph, write about how this place looks from the outside; in the second paragraph, go to the inside, moving through the haunted place. Make your writing as atmospheric as you can.

Remind students that there needs to be some kind of bridge created between the descriptions of the outside and the inside. Ask students to brainstorm about how transitions might work. For example, the narrator might start walking inside a house or building at the end of paragraph one, or a huge, supernatural owl might carry the narrator by the scruff of the neck away from a safe mountainside into the forest deep. Discuss how, in a story, a bridge needs to be subtly built; using phrases such as "on the other hand" would break the mood.

Warm Up: This assignment can be great fun for students; it works especially well if you read them something scary, such as Edgar Allan Poe's "The Raven" or a few paragraphs from "The Fall of the House of Usher." This gets their brains tingling with mysterious, gothic vocabulary words. You might have students call out great spooky words and write them on the board (*gloom, gloaming, murky, wretched, spoiled, ruined, lost, mournful, pale, ghostly, deathly, chill, odd, eerie, foggy, dusk, apparition*, and so on).

Follow Up: Students love to read these sorts of pieces aloud. You can use their work to celebrate Halloween without chaos or sugar-induced madness. Carve out enough time so that all volunteers can read.

IN ORDER

Skills Focus: to use transitions to show sequence

Assignment: Follow the directions on *Unscramble the Sentences* to complete the activity.

Provide each student with copies of pages 32–33. Tell them to:

1. First identify the two topics. Divide the sentences into two groups, labeling them A and B.

2. Determine the topic sentence and the concluding sentence for each group.

3. On a separate piece of paper, put the paragraphs together again. Remind them to pay close attention to the flow of logic. Watch for key words like *so* and *however*.

In the box on page 28 are the sentences put back together as they were originally written. Have students look at the structure of the paragraphs. Discuss with them the transitional device the writer used.

Answer Key

Reginald McSneer only appears to be a good candidate for Mayor of the Arts; in reality he is a dull-witted person who thinks only of junk food and talk TV. On the street, however, we see him parading around town in a tweed suit and French beret, peering "intelligently" through glasses, pretending to care about the arts and the welfare of our citizens. If you catch him at home, will he be reading or listening to music? He will not. No, he will be home, on the couch, singing along with commercials for hamburgers. On voting day, you must firmly, soundly, without regret, pull the lever and reject lazy boy Reginald McSneer and instead vote yes for Bahiyah the Lovely.

Bahiyah deserves every vote in this town because time and again she has demonstrated her love of the arts. A student of drums, a painter of watercolors, a fan of museums, Bahiyah has already made the arts her life. While others crave dinner, she craves poetry. If you hum a commercial jingle to her, she will stare at you blankly because she watches TV, but only once in a while. Bahiyah has volunteered in the Youth Center, teaching painting for free. She painted the door of City Hall with a mural depicting a choir of town children. In City Hall we need someone like Bahiyah, not only adorning its outer gateways, but directing its inner halls. So vote for Bahiyah the Lovely on November third and make a major change in the Office of the Arts.

CRAFTING TRANSITIONS

Skills Focus: to practice using transitional techniques

Assignment: Write two different topic sentences to follow The Snowflake Institute paragraph. In one, repeat a key word to create the transition; in another, use a transitional expression. Pick the one you like best and then write a paragraph about an imaginary, terrible ski school called "Alps Are Us." Make up all the details but write in the same tone as the first paragraph; they should go together well.

Copy the following paragraph on the board for students.

> The Snowflake Institute of Safe Skiing provides the best winter-sport instruction around. While other ski schools merely slap skis on you and teach you the snow plow, the Snowflake Institute recognizes that getting on a ski lift safely the first day may be challenge enough for many a skier. More than once, the new skier at Alps Are Us has been knocked over on his or her face and forced to eat a huge and humiliating mouthful of snow. At The Snowflake Institute, the skiing process is broken down into steps so that by the end of a week, a new skier can put on ski boots and skis, ride a lift, and ski down the beginners' slopes without fear.

Warm Up: Have students look at the tone and intention of the paragraph about The Snowflake Institute. What is the writer trying to do? Why is the writer writing it? Does he or she have a bias? Who is the implied audience for the paragraph?

Follow Up: Have students write two paragraphs that make a comparison between two elements (restaurants, toys, books, and so on). Tell them to work to make a clear transition between the two paragraphs.

FOLLOW UP

Skills Focus: to make smooth transitions between paragraphs

Assignment: Follow the directions on *Follow Up* to complete the writing activity.

Provide each student with a copy of page 34. Tell them to first think carefully. What is the subject? What is the tone of the writing? What kinds of topics could logically follow this paragraph? Tell them their writing style should imitate the style of this paragraph as much as possible. Finally tell them to choose a favorite transitional/topic sentence and write a paragraph that could logically follow this one.

TV WATCHING—THE PROS AND CONS

Skills Focus: to make an analysis

Assignment: Write two paragraphs that address and detail the pros and cons of watching television. Do not take a stand on whether or not watching television is good or bad.

Warm Up: In this assignment you want students to make lists of pros and cons before they begin writing. Then tell them to write two paragraphs. They should link the paragraphs together carefully, creating a smooth transition. Have them refer to *Transitions* (page 31) remind them about transitional words and phrases. To focus students on beginning their paragraphs in an interesting way, write the following sentence on the board: "Eating too many sweets is bad for you." Ask them to revise and embellish the sentence to create a more complex opening line.

Teaching Tip

Note-taking can be very important in writing. You might spot-check students' work to be sure they have taken notes. Do not let them simply compile a list in their heads.

Follow Up: A natural way to enrich this assignment is hold a debate in class. Write this sentence on the board:

Televisions should be locked up when adults are not home.

After the debate, have students discuss how writing the paragraphs prepared them to debate. Lead them to the idea that the writing process can help us clarify our thoughts. Point out that discussing and debating ideas can also help clarify our writing; talking over an idea can be useful before writing about a difficult topic.

Transitions

~ What is a transition? ~

A transition is the element that smoothes the leap from one paragraph to the next. The reader should not feel disoriented by a new paragraph; he or she should feel that it all makes sense, that the ideas or elements clearly connect.

~ How are transitions made? ~

The transition is often made in two places: in the concluding sentence of the previous paragraph and in the topic sentence of the next paragraph.

First of all, in the concluding sentence of a paragraph, a writer often points to or sets up the topic of the next paragraph.

Then, in the topic sentence of the next paragraph, the writer refers directly or indirectly to the topic of the previous paragraph. You can integrate key words or phrases from the concluding sentence into your topic sentence. You can also make this connection with a transitional word.

~ Transitional Words and Phrases ~

likewise	similarly	have in common
in the same way	different	on the contrary
on the other hand	however	instead
conversely	whereas	unlike
both	unlike	consequently
as a result	caused by	but
for this reason	also	because of

Unscramble the Sentences

The sentences below are for two related paragraphs, but they are scrambled and out of order. Your job is to put the sentences and paragraphs back together again.

∾ Sentences ∾

Reginald McSneer only appears to be a good candidate for Mayor of the Arts; in reality he is a dull-witted person who thinks only of junk food and talk TV.

If you hum a commercial jingle to her, she will stare at you blankly because she watches TV, but only once in a while.

On voting day, you must firmly, soundly, without regret, pull the lever and reject lazy boy Reginald McSneer and instead vote yes for Bahiya the Lovely.

While others crave dinner, she craves poetry.

Bahiyah deserves every vote in this town because time and again she has demonstrated her love of the arts.

On the street, however, we see him parading around town in a tweed suit and French beret, peering "intelligently" through glasses, pretending to care about the arts and the welfare of our citizens.

So vote for Bahiyah the Lovely on November third and make a major change in the Office of the Arts.

If you catch him at home, will he be reading or listening to music?

A student of drums, a painter of watercolors, a fan of museums, Bahiyah has already made the arts her life.

Unscramble the Sentences (continued)

He will not.

Bahiyah has volunteered in the Youth Center, teaching painting for free.

No, he will be home, on the couch, singing along with commercials for hamburgers.

She painted the door of City Hall with a mural depicting a choir of town children.

In City Hall we need someone like Bahiyah, not only adorning its outer gateways, but directing its inner halls.

Follow Up

Read the paragraph below and then compose three transitional sentences for the next paragraph. You will need to think of an appropriate topic for the next paragraph.

Life in the big city has so many merits that it may be hard to name them all, but, really, it is the liveliness of city dwellers and the ideas they generate that provide a city with its special glow and capacity for growth. What makes a city unique varies, but nearly all cities are associated with business, innovation, the arts, and ethnic diversity. From New York City to Chicago to Seattle, people will stand in line to see plays, art shows, and concerts; people are interested in things outside themselves. The streets bustle with all kinds of people and all kinds of activity and creativity, though admittedly, not everything that people do in a city is laudable or good. Still, even the buildings are often awe-inspiring; architecture is just another testament to the amazing power of the human mind. Perhaps Samuel Johnson spoke for all cities when he said of his favorite grand town, "When a man is tired of London, he is tired of life." Cities are for those with untiring spirit.

Write three transitional topic sentences.

1. _____

_____

2. _____

_____

3. _____

_____

On a separate sheet of paper or on the back of this sheet, write the next paragraph. Be sure to start your paragraph with one of the sentences you wrote above. Finally, write a fitting title your two-paragraph composition.

Part 3

FULL Compositions

FALLEN HERO

Skills Focus: to develop a personal essay

Assignment: Sometimes people we admire disappoint us: we learn that they are only human. Write about a time when you learned that someone you admired had "feet of clay." How did you see this person before the disappointment? What brought about the change? Did you learn anything about people in general from this experience?

Ask students to give this assignment some thought. This person could be someone they know personally, like a friend or family member, or it could be someone in the public eye.

Provide students with a copy of *The Essay* (page 56). After discussing the form of an essay, have them look at the assignment question. You want them to learn to respond to the full scope of the question. Based on the question, ask them how they might organize such a discussion. What might the different paragraphs be about? For instance, students might use a whole paragraph to explain how the person had been idealized and why. Emphasize that they should fully address the topic. Two possible outlines they might consider appear below. You can write them up on the board for students' consideration. If they have different ideas about how to proceed, encourage them to experiment, but ask what they are considering doing to see if it sounds worthwhile.

Possible Essay Outlines:

A. The first outline below is based on the classic essay structure. This outline would help a student address the question in a full way and give them a sense of how to proceed. If you have students who need to work on structure and idea development, this outline would be helpful.

    I. Introduction: the subject of the composition
   II. Why he or she was idealized
  III. The source and nature of the disappointment
  IV. What the student learned about idealizing people

B. The outline might look like this:

    I. A vignette that tells the story of a disappointment
   II. How and why the person had been idealized
  III. Why this disappointment was so upsetting
  IV. What was learned through this experience

Follow Up: This essay is a natural occasion for students to share with each other. You might ask students to listen for the structure each writer used and to see if they can describe how the essay was organized and if it addressed the topic completely. Discuss with the class what it means here specifically and in general to address a topic fully.

FAMILY PHOTOGRAPH

Skills Focus: to build storytelling skills

Assignment: In this piece, you'll write about your family. Begin with an interesting, important, or evocative family photo. Ruminate on this picture, on what it reveals, and how it makes you feel.

Talk with students about how to approach this assignment. For instance, they may want to discuss the day the picture was taken. Tell students to try to write at least two pages, but emphasize that they shouldn't keep writing if they have nothing more to say. Students should choose pictures with stories or a sense of mystery behind them. They may want to use more formal pictures, but sometimes those odd, informal, or discarded photos no one ever sees are more interesting to think about.

Teaching Tip

Avoid being overly prescriptive about the form this piece should take; students need to work on discovering form, too. Let them use their instincts and see what happens. If someone asks for a suggestion on how to begin, ask other students for ideas.

Follow Up: This is an assignment students are often quite eager to read aloud. Since students will be reading about their families, remind the class of the value of being receptive and generous.

AUTOBIOGRAPHY

Skills Focus: to use vignettes in a composition

Assignment: Write the story of your life until this point. From reading your composition, we should have a good sense of the circumstances of your life (where and how you have lived). We should also hear about some of your favorite and/or important memories from different times in your life.

Tell students that they do not have to include everything; they should focus on what they think is important or representative. The whole composition may contain one or more vignettes. These will provide the reader with a vivid sense of the writer's story.

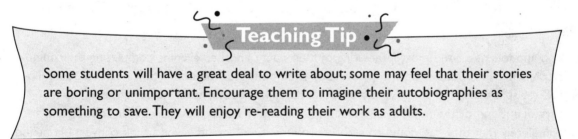

Teaching Tip

Some students will have a great deal to write about; some may feel that their stories are boring or unimportant. Encourage them to imagine their autobiographies as something to save. They will enjoy re-reading their work as adults.

Follow Up: Students will certainly enjoy sharing these stories, so do have them read their autobiographies aloud. You also might read aloud childhood passages from a wonderful memoir such as Frank McCourt's *Angela's Ashes*, James McBride's *The Color of Water*, Isaac Bashevis Singer's *A Day of Pleasure*, Roald Dahl's *Boy*, or Eudora Welty's *One Writer's Beginnings*.

VARIETY IS THE SPICE OF LIFE

Skills Focus: to avoid repetition

Assignment: Follow the directions to complete *Variety is the Spice of Life*.

Provide each student with a copy of page 57. Have them follow the directions to complete the page.

Warm Up: Begin by asking students to listen to the following paragraph (or copy it on the blackboard). Ask them to think about what's wrong with it.

> Bob went with Joe to the store. Bob and Joe bought some shoe polish. Bob and Joe went home. They polished all the shoes. The shoes were shiny again. Bob and Joe then made dinner. Dinner was very dull and bland. They made spaghetti again. Spaghetti was the only dish they ever ate. Bob and Joe were very silly and dull themselves. One day a girl named Louise arrived.

Help them to see that the paragraph contains three common writing mistakes: 1) Unnecessary repetition of key nouns: If the writer made good clear use of pronouns, the paragraph would sound better. 2) All of the sentences are the same length. The repetitive rhythm is tiring and dull. 3) The language is flat. Nothing is described vividly.

To convey the same information more concisely really takes fewer words. Read the following revised paragraph to show how the same information can be conveyed more concisely.

> Bob and Joe went to the store to buy shoe polish. When they returned home, they shined all the shoes and then made their usual dinner of spaghetti. The pasta was dull and bland, just like Bob and Joe, but this changed when Louise arrived.

To make the information interesting, you would need to enliven the paragraph's tone and add details.

> Bob and Joe, never the most interesting of men, spent another evening completing their mind-crushingly dull routine. Go to the store, buy shoe polish. Come home, polish shoes. Make dinner, eat spaghetti. They spent whole beautiful days like robots, never noticing the apple-crisp days of autumn or the mellow days of summer. Routine had trapped them for so long and so completely that they had come to embody routine. One day, however, a pink convertible pulled up their driveway, and a girl stepped out: Louise.

PLAYING WITH SENTENCES

Skills Focus: to use different kinds of sentences to make writing livelier

Assignment: Follow the directions to complete *Playing with Sentences*.

Remind students of the importance of sentence variety by reading the first Bob and Joe paragraph from the *Variety is the Spice of Life* lesson above. Provide each student with copies of pages 58–59. Have them follow the directions to complete the page. Encourage volunteers to read their sentences aloud.

SHEER EXCITEMENT

Skills Focus: to write sentences in a vivid and interesting way

Assignment: Write about the most exciting thing that ever happened to you. Choose words and write sentences that really convey how exciting it was to you so that the reader feels excited too.

Urge students to try to connect to that feeling of excitement before they start writing; they want to get in the mood. Gently nudge them to choose the most vivid, descriptive words as possible in their compositions.

Warm Up: On the board rewrite and expand on the following sentences with student suggestions. Make them more specific, energetic, and interesting.

For example, "A hot air balloon flew over my house" might become "One hot summer afternoon, just as I was sitting down to drink lemonade in the garden, just as I was going to close my eyes for a nap, a huge hot air balloon sailed right over our backyard, and in it, people were shouting for help."

As they revise, the sentences might become longer or turn into different lengths. They will need to imagine the experience of the speaker. Some sentences for revision:

"My little sister was born in the back of our van."

"My father woke me up and told me we were going on a surprise vacation to Disney World."

"We went to see my favorite singer last night."

WHAT IS?

Skills Focus: to use quotation to shape an essay

Assignment: Study these famous quotations. Choose one that you either agree or disagree with. Write an informal personal essay reflecting on the theme of the quotation. Don't worry too much here about structure, but try to write a page or two. Be sure the reader knows what you think and why you think it.

Quotations:

"...Truth is precious and divine..." —Samuel Butler

"Life is short; live it up." —Nikita Khrushchev

"To thine own self be true." —William Shakespeare

Add any quotations you feel your students would enjoy writing about. Give students at least half an hour to write on their themes. Tell students to introduce the quotation somewhere in the beginning of their compositions. They should stay on the topic and paragraph appropriately, but they should not worry too much about structure. Encourage students to think on paper with this assignment. Has personal experience influenced a response to the statement? Explain to students that they don't necessarily have to come to a conclusion, but they should be specific about their responses and give some examples.

Warm Up: Before students begin to write, spend a few minutes discussing each quotation and what it means. What questions does the quotation raise? If students think truth is "precious," then they should explain why. If students seem hesitant, you might hint at some of the implications of the quotations. For instance, if life is short, should we really live it up? What are the benefits of doing that? What are the dangers?

Follow Up: After you return this set of papers, divide students into three discussion groups based on the quotations. Ask each group to discuss the quotation together and urge them to read sections of their essays aloud to each other. Let students chat with each other informally. Then, while they are still in their groups, ask if anybody heard an idea from another student that they had not thought of. Ask: What makes us respond to the same statement so differently?

BEAUTIFUL DREAMER

Skills Focus: to use a verbal refrain to shape a piece

Assignment: What do you dream about doing and being? Where do you dream about going? What do you hope the future will be like for yourself? for the world? Why do you hope so? In one or two pages, write a series of paragraphs that each begin with the sentence, "I dream" or, "I sometimes dream" or some other variation.

This assignment, which works well in the period around Martin Luther King Jr. Day, is designed to get students to express something of their interior world on paper. Tell them not to worry about being realistic; no one really knows much in advance about what might happen. They can wish for anything on paper.

Warm Up: To get students started with this assignment, ask if any of them know Martin Luther King's famous "I have a dream" speech. Read aloud parts of this speech (or play a recording of it). Then reread it, leaving out the refrain "I have a dream." Discuss the difference in effect the refrain has on the speech.

WHAT'S IN A MEAL

Skills Focus: to focus on creating atmosphere

Assignment: Tell the story of a memorable or holiday meal in your household. Create a sense of an individual occasion and give the particulars: the characters, their conversation, the setting, and the food. Create a strong sense of mood. How did you feel about your family during that meal?

Ask students to focus on creating a sense of atmosphere: the reader should know what it is like to share a holiday meal with each student's family. The reader should smell the aromas from the kitchen, hear the arguments about basting the turkey, and so on. Word choices should reflect the atmosphere they're trying to create. (This assignment works especially well just after Thanksgiving.)

Follow Up: This is a fine assignment for students to revise since the focus is simple. Give students comments that push them to be more detailed or more precise about their feelings: show them the opportunities in their pieces to create a sense of mood. After students revise their work in light of your comments, have them read aloud the revisions. After polishing their writing, they will be eager to share their work.

THE IN-CLASS JOURNAL

Skills Focus: to think on paper

Assignment: Begin keeping a journal. The one requirement for journal keeping is that assignments be done thoughtfully. You can be funny, serious, personal, or sad, but unless the assignment calls for it, avoid being too silly, sloppy, or thoughtless. Your writing here can be informal, but it should still be focused.

You can use journal writing in your class in any number of ways, but make it clear to your students that usually they will be writing in response to questions or topics. Emphasize that this is different from a diary or journal at home where they always determine subject matter.

The journals can simply be a standard-sized spiral notebook: you ask students to bring in their own. Keep the journals in your classroom, and pass them out at appropriate moments, which really can be planned or spontaneous. If you use journal writing over the course of a whole term or year, do find time early to look them over to make sure everyone is on the right track. After that, look them over at regular but not necessarily frequent intervals. You can write responses directly onto each page, or if you want to leave their pages unsullied, devote the last page or two of their journals to a general response section. Make sure your responses are supportive; do not focus on spelling. Tell students what you found interesting; try to converse with them on paper about their ideas. Take them seriously as thinkers: we want to create thinkers.

Note: Occasionally, a student may feel uncomfortable about something personal he or she has written; in that case, reassure the student about your general intentions as a reader. But if the student wants to pull that page out of the notebook, respect his or her wishes. We do not want, however inadvertently, to invade student privacy. Writing freely can lead students to express things they may not have intended to utter. It's better for them to write freely and then edit than to write in a constrained, self-conscious manner. (However, should you read something disturbing or alarming, it may be necessary to involve the appropriate administrator.)

SO FAR AWAY

Skills Focus: to create a believable character

Assignment: You are going to create a character who is far from home, probably feeling very out of place, and trying to get home. Give the reader a very clear sense of who the character is. Also, describe the setting well. You have to invent a character, a place, and an obstacle for the character to overcome so he or she can get home. By the end of the story, it should be clear whether or not that's possible.

Remind students of all the factors that go into who we are: age, sex, ethnicity, class, temperament, family background, and current situation. Someone may normally be easygoing, but food shortages caused by war might bring out something different in that person.

Tell students that the reader should quickly know who the character is and why he or she is away from home. The writer can decide whether or not the character will get to return home; the story does not need to include the actual return home. Some stories may be sad, and some may be happy.

Warm Up: Ask students to think of stories (and movies, if it helps) that involve someone far from home. Some fictional models include Abel in *Abel's Island*, Kit in *The Witch of Blackbird Pond*, or Huck and Jim in *The Adventures of Huckleberry Finn*.

If a student says he or she cannot think of an idea for a story, offer some suggestions (a spoiled kid lost at the mall, a businessman locked in the restroom at a football stadium, and so on). Often a student will not like your suggestions, which encourages the student to think of his or her own idea.

THE PROPHECY

Skills Focus: to develop a strong plot

Assignment: Write a story in which a character hears a prediction about his or her future. This prediction could come from a variety of sources—a fortune cookie, a fortune teller, or a horoscope. The story should involve how this character reacts to and handles the prediction.

For this assignment, remind students to describe things very well. Tell them to focus on letting the reader see people, places, objects, and situations vividly. A reader, for example, should not just see a piece of paper but a particular piece of paper—one that looks like it has some history behind it. Remind students to create a sense of mystery as they write. Predictions, you might tell them, usually involve love, money, family, and/or work.

Warm Up: Ask students why people seek predictions about their futures in the first place. What makes someone want to know what is coming? Tell them they should think about what is happening in the life of the main character before he or she receives the prediction; this might become a part of the story.

Follow Up: Talk to students about the use of a prophecy as a plot device. In classical drama, characters like Sophocles' Oedipus often try to run from prophecies, especially if they don't like what they've heard. For instance, Oedipus hears that he will kill his father, so he leaves home to avoid this. Shakespeare's Macbeth hears that he will be king, and this makes him rush to his future. Huck Finn hears in a "reading" from Jim that his missing and very dangerous father is nearby and is contemplating how to get Huck's money. Huck then "sells" his money to Judge Thatcher to protect it.

CHILDREN'S STORYBOOK

Skills Focus: to focus on plot and to write with a specific audience in mind

Assignment: Write and illustrate a children's story that a four or five year old would love to read. First, come up with your story; think up a good plot. Then, copy it onto blank pages, making room for illustrations.

Explain to students that their pictures can fill in some of the details, but children love to hear wonderful words, too, so they should pick interesting words but ones children would understand. You might want to hint about some story lines to them: a journey, a lost object, looking for an answer to a question, a mystery of some kind, and so on.

Students who don't wish to illustrate their stories could cut out pictures from magazines.

Follow Up: A natural follow up for this is to have students read their stories to a kindergarten or first-grade class (if they share a school building). Or they could read to each other. Finally, if your class has been working hard and needs a luscious treat, have them bring in their favorite children's books from when they were small to read aloud.

NIGHTLIFE

Skills Focus: to establish a setting

Assignment: Write a story of at least three or four paragraphs about the secret nightlife of something in your home. You might write about inanimate objects which, unbeknownst to humans, are actually alive, or about real creatures or invented ones. Invent a whole world that we humans know nothing about. The reader should learn how the night begins, develops, and ends.

Encourage students to be lavishly imaginative here. They could imagine that a set of objects comes to life at night, such as tools in the basement, dirty clothes in the hamper, or silverware in the drawer. They might make up some creatures. Tell students to explain why we humans never see this nightlife. Urge them to think about all the things and animals in their homes. Ask them to think about how certain objects seem to have a personality or even a sense of gender; for example, a fork might seem different from a spoon to them.

Warm Up: Have students close their eyes and picture the room or rooms in their houses where their stories will take place. What are their homes like late at night? What do they sound like when everyone is asleep? Encourage students to consider beginning with descriptions of the houses before the secret nightlives begin.

Follow Up: Students may enjoy hearing portions of *The Borrowers* by Mary Norton, and certainly they will enjoy reading aloud their pieces. Ask them to discuss night as a time in story-telling. What kinds of things take place at night? Also, why is it that some objects seem to have human qualities? Why do we see things this way?

STORY IN A POEM OF SHORT LINES

Skills Focus: to write a poem that tells a story

Assignment: In the poem "Father on Black Ice," Nancy White writes about her father. Write a poem that tells a story about you and one of your parents. The story can involve a simple action or a moment that seems meaningful or momentous for some reason. Your poem should also use very short lines and crisp images that convey a sense of place, mood, and emotion.

Warm Up: Because this very specific assignment can get terrific results, Nancy White's poem from *Sun, Moon, Salt* is presented here in a reproducible form (see pages 60–63); you might show the poem to students before giving them the assignment. Begin by reading the poem with students and talking about White's use of language. What feeling does the poem create with those short lines? What images stand out? What do students think the poem is about? What feeling does the poem convey? What is its tone? What situation does the poem describe? How old do they think the child is? What kinds of poetic devices does it use? Discuss simile and metaphor with students and give examples.

Carefully go over the assignment with students. Point out how visual White's poem is and encourage them to tell their stories in ways that help readers see the scenes very vividly.

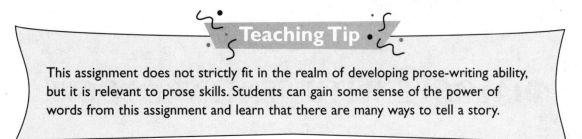

Teaching Tip

This assignment does not strictly fit in the realm of developing prose-writing ability, but it is relevant to prose skills. Students can gain some sense of the power of words from this assignment and learn that there are many ways to tell a story.

Discussion: This assignment is a great time to bring up the difference between poetry and prose. Have students look up these words as part of their homework or do it informally in class.

MYSTERY EGG

Skills Focus: to write with a particular audience in mind

Assignment: Write a story that revolves around the discovery and handling of a strange, unusual-looking egg. Before you begin writing, decide on the audience for the story: a child you know, your mom or dad, a sibling, your best friend, Grandma or Grandpa, or someone else!

Emphasize to the students that their audience will effect the kind of language they choose to use: parents will enjoy something different than young children, and best friends might like something that makes parents roll their eyes. Also, remind them to pay attention to details especially descriptive details about the egg's size, shape, color and markings. And they should create suspense; as they begin, they should make readers curious to know what, if anything, will make the egg hatch and what is inside the egg.

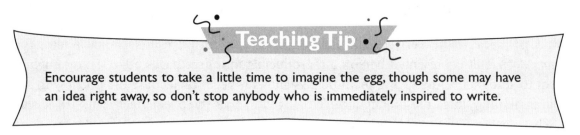

Teaching Tip

Encourage students to take a little time to imagine the egg, though some may have an idea right away, so don't stop anybody who is immediately inspired to write.

Follow Up: Because this is written with an audience in mind, students could polish their stories and present them as gifts. Students could revise, perfect the spelling and punctuation, design a cover and give their story as a holiday or birthday present.

William Styron wrote a wonderfully funny story called "Benjy" that you might want to read to students some time after you complete the project.

DIALOGUE WITH SENTENCE FOCUS

Skills Focus: to use correct dialogue form

Assignment: Write a story that involves an argument between two people who are very different. One character should use long sentences; the other character should use short sentences. By the end of the story the argument should be resolved. Your story should be one-and-a-half to two pages.

The stories will mostly be dialogue, although students can add some descriptive or expositional passages. The effect here may be comic if the students like; encourage them to create an "odd couple" of some sort. Students should imagine very precise but different individuals who would be likely to use language in ways distinct from each other. Insisting that students resolve the argument will require them to bring their stories to some kind of satisfying end—at least for the reader. Urge them to write at least two pages. This assignment will take a minute or two to explain; you might consider trying it yourself first, just to be sure you understand how it works.

Warm Up: Review punctuation of dialogue and how to place the speaker tags in different sections of a sentence.

> Franky said, "I hate liver and onions."
> "You don't hate it," said his mother. "You just may not like it."
> "Oh no. I hate it, all right," he said.
> "Franklin, if you don't stop saying that this instant," she said, "there will be no soccer practice for you."

Follow Up: Have students read aloud their work. Discuss the relationship between sentence length and character. How do we speak when we are in certain moods, for example, when we're tired and upset or full of energy and angry? or when we're being sarcastic?

∴ FINDERS KEEPERS ✏

Skills Focus: to use play structure

Assignment: Using dramatic form, write a scene for a play in which something is hidden or lost. Your characters are in search of whatever the thing is.

After students think this assignment over for a minute or two, generate a discussion about what questions they might need to consider. First of all, who is in the scene? Where is it taking place? What is missing and what happened to it? Finally, encourage students to imagine each character individually; they should not all sound alike.

Warm Up: Show examples of a play's format on the board. Point out that each character's name is capitalized. Stage directions appear in parentheses.

> JEFFREY: If I don't find my soccer ball, Mom won't let me go to practice. (He looks under his bed.)
>
> MICHAEL: Are you sure you didn't eat it with all those cookies?
>
> JEFFREY: Ha ha. (Jeffrey sticks out his tongue.)
>
> MICHAEL: I'll see you after practice. (Looking smug, he puts on his cleats.)

Follow Up: Encourage students to read aloud or even perform their scenes. They may need to make copies of their scenes if there are more than two characters. Performing their scenes will help students hear their writing. Some may be surprised; a character may sound flat, or the audience might laugh at something unexpected. Tell them that a playwright often does not know if a scene works until he or she hears it read aloud.

CONFESS!

Skills Focus: to write a first-person narrative

Assignment: Write a first-person narrative in which a character confesses to having done something. It could be something major, like a crime, or something minor. The story can be in the form of a letter, a testimony, or a monologue, or you can imagine that the character is confessing to someone such as a police officer, a family member, or a religious leader.

The nature of the confession is up to the students, but remind them that it does not have to be a crime per se. It can simply be something about which the character feels conflicted, such as being in love. The narrator might be very eager to confess or might be more reluctant, but by the end of the story, the reader should know what the character did and why. Delaying the confessions will very likely result in more suspenseful stories. Encourage students to conceive unexpected narrators; suggest they develop characters who are completely unlike themselves.

Follow Up: Many stories have a confessional quality. In fact St. Augustine's *Confessions* influenced the early writers of novels. Ask students if they can think of stories or movies with a confessional quality. You might want to read them some Edgar Allan Poe. Much of his work, "The Cask of Amontillado," for example, has a strongly confessional quality. And students will certainly enjoy sharing their own stories.

STREAM OF CONSCIOUSNESS

Skills Focus: to develop a voice

Assignment: Write about anything on your mind until I tell you to stop. Do not think about paragraphing, spelling, or grammar. Write as quickly as you can; try to set down on paper everything that you're thinking.

Assure students that they don't need to make transitions or establish topics. They can pick one of the sentences below to start with, and if they get stuck, they can select another one. Or if students get stuck, they should keep repeating their last word until a new thought or image comes to them. Write the following prompts on the board:

> I always remember . . .
> I always think about . . .
> I hate . . . I wish I could . . .
> I dreamt last night about . . .
> I'm feeling . . .

Note: The role of this assignment is very intentionally to free students from structured writing assignments and to experience generating ideas and language in a freewheeling way. It will remind students of how much they can write and acquaint them with how rich their interior worlds are. Give students about thirty minutes to write.

Follow Up: Ask students to discuss what kinds of things they wrote about. Lead them in a discussion of how writing in itself can reveal our thoughts and teach us about ourselves. It also can bring us to interesting ideas and images for stories and poems. Finally, looking at the raw material created by doing stream-of-consciousness writing, discuss this kind of expressive writing. How does it differ from editing and shaping a piece? How much should a writer edit his or her thoughts and words while writing? What is the danger if a writer is too careful about what he or she says?

SAME THEME, DIFFERENT READER

Skills Focus: to experiment with diction

Assignment: Write about the same topic in two ways, in two different paragraphs, for two different audiences. In the first paragraph, use formal diction; in the second, use informal diction. Describe something you have done recently—perhaps going to the doctor or trying out for a sports team or a play.

Discuss diction with students so you are certain they understand what it means. Read the following sentences to them:

> "Now we will check out why it's always winter in Narnia."

> "Johnny Tremain is pretty obnoxious."

> "Hamlet is nuts."

Help students to see that the informal, colloquial style of these sentences is inappropriate for a formal essay.

Warm Up: On the board write strong, complex topic sentences for two different paragraphs. One paragraph is for the principal, the other is for a student. The topic could be, for example, the food in the school cafeteria or the color of the school walls.

AN ESSAY ON MEANING

Skills Focus: to revise an essay

Assignment: In a well-developed essay of roughly four paragraphs, agree or disagree with the following statement by the Spanish writer Cervantes: "Honesty is the best policy." In the body of your essay, use examples from your own life or from literature, history, or current events to explain your thinking.

This assignment has three steps as follows:

1. Give the quotation to students to think about as homework. Ask them to jot down notes. Explain that they are going to write on the topic the next day.

2. Have students write in class on this topic for thirty to forty-five minutes. Remind them that they should take a clear stand in this essay: their perspectives should be clear in their introductions. Students should explain their responses; giving clear examples here is very important. They should write quickly and clearly.

3. For homework, have students edit their own essays using red pens. Then they should recopy the essays, correcting all errors. Encourage students to alter their arguments if necessary. They should hand in the first and second drafts the next day.

Follow Up: This is an assignment you want to mark carefully. After they hand in their paragraphs, ask students how many of them found real errors in their first drafts. Assure students that this is normal: when writing quickly, we do make mistakes. Revising allows us to improve our work dramatically; nearly all fine writers have to rework significantly before their writing really shines.

PLEASE CHANGE

Skills Focus: to write a formal letter

Assignment: In a formal letter addressed to an individual or organization, write about something that needs changing. Explain not only what should change and why but also how it should change. Give some suggestions.

Suggest to students that they can make this letter about any number of things: striking sports players or organizations, city ordinances concerning young people, television programming, national affairs, or the rising price of cheeseburgers or toys. Tell students that in a formal letter, the purpose of the letter should be clear from the first paragraph.

Warm Up: To help students understand proper form, go over the *A Formal Letter* reproducible (page 64) with them. Point out what information is included in a letter, why it is there, and where everything properly goes. If they write their letters on notebook paper, have them skip a couple of lines between the different elements: heading, inside address, salutation, text, closing, and signature. Stress that their letters should look clean and approachable. Finally, before students begin, ask them to explain why a writer should use formal English in a business letter.

Follow Up: You might encourage students to send their letters, in which case you might want to have them do final drafts based on your comments. Teach them how to address a letter. Some students will probably receive responses, which will reinforce the idea that writing is useful in the real world.

Note: Often students who have trouble with spatial/visual work will have trouble sorting out how to place things on the page; they may need some monitoring. Have younger students or those especially inexperienced with language copy the letter on the reproducible on page 64 before they do the assignment.

JOB APPLICATION

Skills Focus: to write a letter for a job

Assignment: Imagine that you're applying for a job. For the purposes of this assignment, use a pencil to write a letter of inquiry. Explain which job you're interested in, describe your qualifications, and list your references. Give some thought in advance as to how you will paragraph.

Possible jobs and addresses:

Assistant camp counselor
    Apply to:
    Mabel Pearson,
    Director Long Pine Camp
    Route 1
    Littletown, Wyoming 86130

Summer babysitter: Apply to:
    Mr. and Mrs. Friendly
    Carson Road
    Santa Fe, New Mexico 60329
Bus boy: Apply to:
    Kwame Lewis, Manager
    Big Plates Restaurant
    49126 Oyster Drive
    Sloughton, Louisiana 01293

Deejay: Apply to:
    Joanna Justice, President
    Spinning Discs 1111
    Sweetbriar Drive
    Detroit, Michigan 02938

Have students select one of the jobs above or let them make up their own. Tell them that they can invent the particulars as long as they use letter form accurately and write formally. Remind students to sign their letters!

Follow Up: Before students hand in their letters, divide the class into pairs. Partners should look over each other's letters and check form, clarity, and spelling. They should make suggestions to each other, but first remind them to offer advice tactfully. Students should then use these suggestions to make any necessary changes in their letters. Let them know that when they need to make a good impression, they should let someone with an informed eye check their work.

THE FOOD CRITIC

Skills Focus: to make and organize an evaluation

Assignment: You have been hired by a publication to write a review of a restaurant. Your review should provide clear guidance to prospective diners about the quality of the restaurant. The tone of your review is up to you, but write in the first person.

You must describe the place and the food in elaborate detail. Your readers should learn the following from your review:

* ★ name of restaurant
* ★ location

- ★ atmosphere
- ★ service
- ★ dress code
- ★ type of food and its quality
- ★ particularly good or bad dishes
- ★ price range
- ★ level of formality
- ★ your rating

Warm Up: This assignment integrates many skills, so use a two-part warm-up.

1. Focus students' attention on the list of elements that the review must include and talk about how they might organize their reviews. Some of the information is simply data: should they lead with that? Would that make an interesting opening? After you establish that the writer has an organizational dilemma, show them one solution many critics use: they create a box of useful facts that contains location, price range, dress code, type of food, and rating. This makes important information easily accessible and allows the writer to critique the food and service in the text of the review.

2. Discuss with students how the tone of a publication would influence how they write. A review in a magazine for teenagers would probably be different from a review in a major newspaper. As a class, come up with a list of different publications for which students could imagine writing restaurant reviews. They could also create imaginary publications; for example, maybe someone wants to write for an imaginary magazine called *Snap* for kids or teenagers who love music and dance, or for *Vault*, a magazine for middle school gymnasts. In addition to tone, students need to think about diction. Given the publication, should their language be formal or informal?

Note: While it may be tempting to force students to write their reviews using formal diction, keep in mind that a good part of what you are doing here is educating them about the idea of audience and employing language appropriate to a given occasion. When students actually go through that process of writing for an audience, they begin to internalize the concept of diction.

Follow Up: Consider making a booklet of these reviews (this idea is more practical if you and your students have access to computers). You could also make a website with them.

BLUEPRINT FOR THE FUTURE

Skills Focus: to make and use an outline

Assignment: Write a four- or five-paragraph essay about something that you believe needs improvement. Propose changes. You could write about your hometown, a sport, school, television, food, a restaurant, a store, main street, and so on. Your subject should be something you really care about.

Warm Up: Talk first about the introduction. By the end of the first paragraph, the reader should know what the problem is and, in general, the solutions the student will address in detail in the essay. On the board, outline the probable course of such an essay as shown below. Have students copy the outline. You want to steer them to the following idea: The human mind likes things to make sense. In their essays, they will simply be explaining problems and how to fix them.

    I. What's wrong and what can be done
    II. The full scope of the problem, how it came about and why it is so bad
   III. The solution
   IV. An additional solution (optional paragraph)
    V. Conclusion: Why it's so important to solve this problem, what's at stake,
       and why there's room for hope

Follow Up: Have students revise their essays based on your comments. In your comments, pay close attention to their transitions.

·. · HALLOWEEN REFLECTION

Skills Focus: to organize and outline ideas

Assignment: In a five-paragraph essay, discuss the merits of three kinds of candy. In the body of your paper, devote a full paragraph to a description of each kind of candy. How does it taste? What does it look like? Is it colorful? How long does it last? Be very detailed: we should see and taste the candy. Make the reader want a piece! In the conclusion of your essay, and not before, identify which candy is best.

This frivolous topic uses a formal approach and works especially well when candy is king: at Halloween. Tell students to describe lavishly, even to the point of absurdity if they want, as long as they keep their language formal. The reader should be able to visualize and experience how each piece of candy looks and tastes.

Warm Up: Have students begin by outlining this on a sheet of paper. Have them look at *The Essay* on page 56. In the outline, they should order their discussion. Ask students to give some thought to where they should discuss the best candy. Should it come first? last? in the middle? Emphasize that there is no right answer.

Note: You may find that some students may not want to write about candy, although many will find this fun. If they want to write about three sports, three cookies, three video games or three whatever, consider allowing a change of focus; this won't violate the purpose of the assignment.

THE LITERARY ESSAY

Skills Focus: to use the text as evidence

Assignment: In a four- to five-paragraph essay, use proper essay form to write a response to the following question: _____. In the body of your essay, be sure to use examples and quotations from the text to back up your thesis.

Keeping topics sharply focused and accessible works well with students new to the literary essay. Pose a sharply focused question that will push them to create a thesis. One successful type of question asks students to examine changes a character undergoes from the beginning to the end of a book. Asking students to compare characters can also be very effective.

Warm Up: Use the question for some prewriting work. Write the question on the board and tell students to rewrite it as a statement on a sheet of paper, building an answer into the end of the statement. Use a different question to illustrate such as, Why are the Olympics important? The Olympics are important because they build international good will in a strife-torn world. Ultimately, students can rephrase this statement in their own words when they write their essays.

Urge students to think about the order of the essay. Especially with more inexperienced students, discuss how they might outline. In the case of an essay about a change in a character, you might suggest the following four-paragraph outline:

    I. Introduction: how the character changes
    II. The character early in the book
   III. The character later in the book
   IV. Conclusion

Remind students that they need to find evidence in the book to back up their points. If you break the essay process into steps, consider assigning the collection of evidence as homework for one night. Remind students to record page numbers.

Be sure to give students ample time to do a good job with this assignment.

Follow Up: When you feel your students are ready, have them write second drafts of their essays. Explain to them the place of revision in polishing work. With an eye to student revision, make comments on their papers, looking especially at three things: Is there a thesis? Did they use evidence? Do their paragraphs have topic sentences? Tell students to revise their essays, and have them turn in both drafts. Make sure their revisions have responded to your comments.

The Essay

A formal essay or composition is a focused, developed discussion of a well-defined topic, which is called a thesis. An essay explains and validates your thesis with convincing examples.

An essay, like a paragraph, has an orderly shape. It has three parts—a beginning, a middle, and an end:

～ Essay Structure ～

I. Introductory Paragraph
This paragraph contains the thesis. The thesis defines your topic and tells what you will cover in the essay.

II. Body: The Internal Paragraphs
In these paragraphs, you explain and give details to support your thesis. Like a lawyer, you need to give evidence to back up your thesis, and you need to provide it in an orderly manner.

III. Concluding Paragraph
In this paragraph, you wrap up your discussion and leave the reader feeling satisfied by the conclusion.

～ Tips for Writing Essays ～

1) Come up with a precise thesis. Don't confuse topic with thesis. For example, "Computers are important." is a topic. "Computers have changed the lives of teachers and students forever." is a thesis. A precise thesis gives you something to prove.

2) Find identifying examples to back up your thesis. You may need to do research, interview people, or think of personal experiences from your own life to find good examples.

3) Organize your ideas in an outline. Following an outline will keep your essay focused.

4) REMEMBER TO PROOFREAD FOR SPELLING AND PUNCTUATION ERRORS!

Name _____ Date _____

Variety Is the Spice of Life

Rewrite the paragraph below twice. Use the back of this sheet if necessary.

1) First rewrite it to make it less repetitive. Use pronouns where you can and play with sentence variety. Make sure the sentences are not the same length. Combine sentences if you wish.

2) Then rewrite it using a livelier tone.

Add details to make the story come to life. Create a sense of suspense and make the writing more interesting.

The house stood on Adams Street. All the children played there each day. The children liked to ride their bikes there. The children liked to skateboard there. The children liked to play kickball there. The children sometimes fought. Sometimes they played together well. One day the children discovered something scary on Adams Street.

_____

_____

_____

_____

_____

_____

_____

_____

_____

_____

Playing With Sentences

Good writers use different kinds of sentences. Look at the examples of sentence types below and then imitate the type of sentence. Write a complete sentence on the lines.

1. Some sentences use a form of *when* and *then*.

> "When the last leaves have fallen and the first snow flies, then Minnesotans know it is time to put on the snow tires."

Write your own sentence that uses a *when/then* construction.

_____

_____

_____

2. Some sentences begin with *To*.

> "To be or not to be, that is the question."
> "To err is human; to forgive divine."

Write a sentence beginning with *To love:* _____

_____

_____

3. Some sentences create a strong sense of contrast:

> The early days of summer were light and sweet and warm, but the final days were humid and scorching and sad.

Create a strong sense of contrast by completing the following sentence:

Semu has always loved school and even loved buying school supplies, but Jerome

_____

_____

_____

Playing With Sentences (continued)

4. Some sentences open with a series of three nouns or adjectives.

　　Salty, hot, and wet, her tears tasted oddly good.
　　June, July, and August, these months are student favorites.

Complete the following sentence.

Funny, intelligent, and good looking _____

_____

_____

_____

5. Some sentences reverse the usual order of words.

　　"Over the river and through the woods to Grandmother's house we go."

Write a sentence that begins, "With school coming on and summer coming to an end, with her hair growing out and her best friend having moved"

_____

_____

_____

6. Some sentences use an *if/then* construction. Sometimes the word *then* is implied.

　　If the river rises, then the farm will be flooded.
　　If we hurry, we won't be late.

Write a sentence that begins, "If the time comes when there is no more television" _____

_____

_____

_____

Father on Black Ice

We step onto the lake, empty

platter of white.

Dark huts dot

the drifted, scalloped

vastness, huts

of the regular men.

We go way

out and dig,

leather mittens lapping

the snow. The ice below

is a black

mirror, black as

an animal's eye!

I am sure we

have found something new

that no one else

knows, not men in huts, not

Mom or my sister

home at the tiny

stove in the play-

room. He tries

to explain: "Vision

is just our eye

taking in reflected

light." What

Father on Black Ice (continued)

is he talking about?
"Watch." He drills with
the auger and shavings
of ice twist
up, clear or white in
the sun. Not black. My life
is heaven and hell and
I am almost
twelve and there are fish
in the dark like backwards
stars below us. Can
they breathe?
What do they
eat? What makes it
worthwhile to go
on living in
such circumstances?
Are there weeds
to brush against?
Sleek, bright, even,
under the lid of shadow,
long and tapering,
maybe shifting to
ease the doubts
or kinks in their drowsing

Father on Black Ice (continued)

panels of flesh for

no soothing

currents could persist under

such a hand as this

ice. Among them our lines

go down. Do they see

a hook as a shard

of light when it drops,

a way out of darkness without

edge or measure? We catch

them. They drip and

flap when we lift

them into the silver air.

Gills flare, gashed

red. The slick jewels

of their eyes. He

catches me

pouring cups of water

over them, filling

the gills to make them

live. He

knows, so

he shows me how to kill.

One thumb in the mouth,

bend the backbone till

Father on Black Ice (continued)

it snaps. Feel it
go? It is cruel
what they feed us,
that we eat. "You will not always
be so unhappy."
He promises.
I want him to
say more, want
to ask him, "Who am
I to you, now
you have pulled me
from the hole
and let me live?"

—Nancy White, from *Sun, Moon, Salt*

A Formal letter

2468 Blippity Blop Road
Car City, Ohio 09861
(heading)

April 1, 2001 *(date)*

Floyd Pickerson *(inside address)*
Chief Executive Officer
STOP Signs USA
5678 Corporate Drive
Yawnley, Alaska 12345

Dear Mr. Pickerson: *(salutation)*

I have noticed that all of the stop signs in my town and in every town are red. I recognize that this is the traditional color, but I would like to say, with all due respect, that we in America, here in the new millennium, could use a change of pace. I would like to propose that you change the color of the stop sign to a color most people enjoy: purple. Purple is a vivid color like red, but it is prettier. With a ellow border and yellow lettering, I am sure the signs would be just as easy to see and would also be more attractive by daylight. Since we have to see the signs so often, perhaps they should be nicer for people to look at. *(text)*

Very Truly Yours, *(closing)*

Silly Soundmaker (signature)

Silly Soundmaker